Bedfordshire's Lost Railways

by
Keith Scholey

Standard class 2 2-6-0 No. 78028 approaching Bedford St Johns, 1959.

Text © Keith Scholey, 2003.
First published in the United Kingdom, 2003,
by Stenlake Publishing,
Telephone / Fax: 01290 551122
Printed by Cordfall Ltd, Glasgow, G21 2QA

ISBN 1 84033 271 9

Black Five 4-6-0 No. 44944 approaching Bedford St Johns, 1959.

INTRODUCTION

The first phase of British railway building left Bedfordshire virtually untouched. It is true that the London & Birmingham Railway, completed in 1838, provided a railhead for the county, but its Leighton Station lay just over the Buckinghamshire border from the town proper. However, the London & Birmingham (which became part of the London & North Western Railway in 1846) soon sent out shoots: to the county town in 1846, via its subsidiary the Bedford Railway, and to Dunstable two years later. In 1850 the Great Northern main line cut through the far east of the county.

Although these main lines were important in national terms – they now form the southern sections of the West Coast (ex-London & North Western Railway) and East Coast (ex-Great Northern Railway) main lines – the company which was to dominate the county was the Midland Railway, based in Derby. In 1857 the Midland built southwards from Leicester to connect up with the Great Northern at Hitchin, thus providing access to London for the wealthy provincial company. Although this was initially relatively cheap, as it cut out the need for a separate approach to London, because of operational and financial difficulties the arrangement was to prove unworkable. So the Midland built a London line of its own, which, when it opened in 1868, effectively rendered the section of the old main line from Bedford to Hitchin redundant. It also dashed the hopes of the Great Northern's branch from Hatfield to Luton and Dunstable, opened just a few years earlier. The Midland provided fast express services to London for the county's two major towns, Luton and Bedford.

The other lines in the county were the London & North Western's Bedford to Cambridge line, opened in 1862, and secondly the Midland's Northampton branch of 1872, which formed the last addition to Bedfordshire's railway system.

The later history of Bedfordshire's railway network is easily told. In the 1923 Grouping the Midland and London & North Western were amalgamated into the London, Midland & Scottish Railway (LMS), while the Great Northern became part of the London & North Eastern Railway (LNER). In 1948 the new companies became state property as British Railways, the former LMS lines in the county becoming part of the London Midland Region and the LNER property being administered by the Eastern Region. Exceptionally, the greater part of the Bedford–Cambridge line, an ex-LMS property, was eventually to become part of the Eastern Region. These changes made little impact in terms of service provided. The 1960s, however, saw the network radically pruned.

Today, the rail system is essentially of the through express type, with all three electrified main lines really only serving the larger towns. Except on the Midland main line south of Bedford, there is little commuter traffic. One interesting exception to this picture is the old Bedford branch. Although many times threatened with closure, this remains as a surviving example of the cross-country branch line. With its charming half-timbered stations, some with the traditional low platforms, a journey on this old-timer is well worth taking.

Bedford branch: Bedford St Johns spur

Passenger service withdrawn	14 May 1984	*Station closed*	*Date*
Distance	0.2 miles	Bedford St Johns	14 May 1984
Company	London & North Western		

A view of Bedford Station, later Bedford St Johns, *c.*1875. The building to the right was erected for the line to Cambridge, all traffic previously being accommodated under the overall roof to the left. These buildings were demolished in 1971.

Bedford St Johns, 1914.

Although the Bedford branch is alive and well its long-time terminal has been terminated! The branch was built by the Bedford Railway, a company organised by a consortium of businessmen and landowners backed by the London & North Western Railway which took over the independent company on completion. The initial concern was to bring general passenger and goods traffic to the county town (the brick manufactories, which latterly characterised the branch, were largely a development of the inter-war years of the twentieth century). Bedford St Johns was opened with the line on 17 November 1846 and was always the most important station of the branch. In its earliest days it was even more notable, for as well as being the county town's only station for the first dozen years of its life, it also hosted the Midland Railway from 1857 to 1859 while the Midland Road station was built.

The St Johns station was rendered redundant in 1984 when a spur was laid in to connect with the current main station in Bedford. A replacement platform was opened on the new line and the old station and its approaches are now derelict. By this time the important sidings near the old station, which served a sawmill, a brewery and a petrol depot among others, had of course been closed.

Cambridge branch (Bedford St Johns to Cambridge) *

Passenger service withdrawn	30 December 1967
Distance	30.4 miles
Company	London & North Western

Stations closed	*Date*
Willington	30 December 1967
Blunham	30 December 1967

Stations closed	*Date*
Girtford Halt	17 November 1940
Sandy	30 December 1967
Potton	30 December 1967

* The closed stations on this line that were in Cambridgeshire were Gamlingay, Old North Road and Lord's Bridge.

4-4-0 No. 5249, 'Bellerophon', approaching Sandy from Potton with a 'horse-box race special', April 1929. The former Great Northern main line is on the right.

LMS locomotive No. 5520, 'Sysyphus', departing from Sandy Station with a freight service for Bletchley while a passenger train arrives, April 1929.

This line, about fourteen miles of which were in Bedfordshire, effectively formed the eastward continuation of the London & North Western's Bedford branch. The line's origins lay in local economics, coupled with the strategic intentions of the London & North Western, but was ultimately the culmination of plans to build a direct Oxford–Cambridge railway which dated back to the beginnings of railway development in the locality. The Bedford & Cambridge Railway was rapidly constructed and opened for regular passenger traffic on 7 July 1862. It was lightly built, mostly following the contours of the land with little in the way of earthworks, and was initially single track (the section between Sandy and Cambridge was doubled by 1871). The greatest expense was the bridges required over the River Ouse and the Great Northern main line at Sandy. In part, the route of the Potton & Sandy Tramway was utilised; this light railway, opened for passengers on 25 June 1857, was promoted by local landowner Sir William Peel, son of the famous Robert. The Bedford & Cambridge Railway was merged into the London & North Western in 1865.

Sandy Station, 1928. The former Great Northern Railway platforms, still open, are to the right, while the train on the left is at the ex-London & North Western Railway platform. Note the well-kept gardens for which the station was famous.

Passenger traffic was always relatively light, especially on the stretch between Bedford and Sandy. In an attempt to boost traffic new stations were opened – Willington in 1903 and Girtford Halt in 1938 – but without much effect. There was some long distance travel on the line, but this can never have amounted to much. Nevertheless, the line survived into the diesel era only to be axed a few years later.

Potton Station, looking north, 16 August 1965.

Goods traffic was mainly agricultural except immediately east of Bedford where there were some industrial sidings. An oilseed mill at Blunham and a brickworks at Sandy were rail-connected. Besides these, vegetable growing dominated, particularly large scale greenhouse-based market gardening around Potton. There was also considerable interchange traffic with the Great Northern main line at Sandy. The line was closed for goods in 1966, although some workings to Goldington power station, just east of Bedford, continued for a while. Between Bedford and Sandy the greater part of the line is in use as a country walk, while the trackbed of the eastern section can be traced along almost all of its length.

Dunstable branch (Leighton Buzzard to Dunstable North)

			Date
Passenger service withdrawn	30 June 1962	*Stations closed*	
Distance	6.8 miles	Stanbridgeford	30 June 1962
Company	London & North Western	Dunstable (first)	January 1866

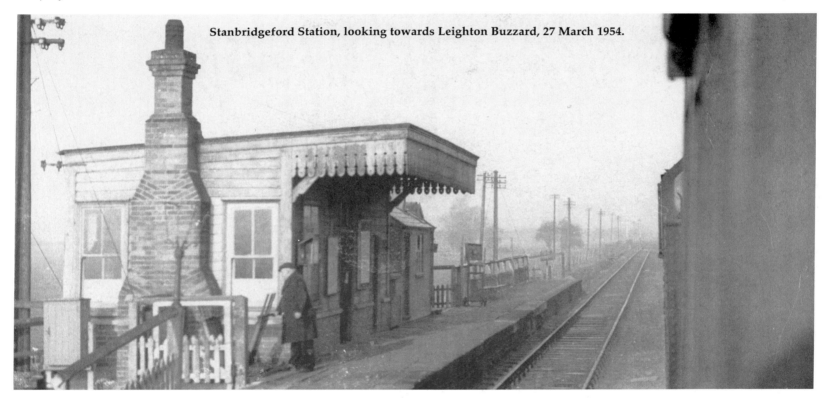

Stanbridgeford Station, looking towards Leighton Buzzard, 27 March 1954.

Soon after the opening of its main line, the London & Birmingham looked around for rapidly growing towns with an eye to profitable branches. Such a town was Luton. However, when the idea was mooted objections were raised about crossing an area of common land outside the town and as a result the line only went as far as Dunstable. The branch to this old coaching town was rapidly constructed and opened on 1 June 1848. By this time the local front company, the Dunstable Branch Railway, had already been merged into the London & Birmingham. The branch featured heavy gradients and was double track throughout. The junction, like most of the London & Birmingham branches, faced north as the goods trade to and from the Midlands was considered more important than that of passengers to London.

Stanbridgeford Station, looking towards Dunstable, 31 July 1960.

In 1858 a junction was made with the Great Northern's Dunstable branch and the original terminal station subsequently closed in January 1866. The new Dunstable Station, opened on a nearby site the same month (it was renamed Dunstable North on 25 September 1950), was owned by the London & North Western but was also the terminus of the Great Northern branch.

Stanbridgeford Station, again facing Dunstable, 15 July 1961.

Essentially the passenger service was a shuttle from Leighton to Dunstable and back. However, certain trains were later to continue on to Luton and for a brief period in the 1880s there were through trains to Bletchley. Except in the earliest years the 'Dunstable Dasher', as the little local train was known, was not particularly well frequented and remained steam hauled until the end. The only intermediate station, Stanbridgeford, served a mixed bag of small villages and was an early addition to the line, being open by 1849.

Stanbridgeford Station, 21 April 1968.

Although there was some general goods traffic, the most important commodities handled were chalk, cement and sand. Much of the latter was from interchange with the Leighton Buzzard Light Railway, a narrow gauge affair which opened in 1919. Stanbridgeford yielded only the products of local market gardening. The line was closed for through goods a year after passenger closure, although a short section as far as Grovebury sidings remained open until the end of the decade. Since closure roadworks have destroyed a large section of the route and much of the rest has been absorbed back into farmland.

Dunstable branch (Hatfield to Dunstable North) *

Passenger service withdrawn	26 April 1965		*Stations closed*	*Date*
Distance	20.4 miles		Dunstable Town	26 April 1965
Company	Great Northern		Chaul End Halt	1919
			Dunstable North	26 April 1965

Stations closed — *Date*
Luton Hoo — 26 April 1965
Luton Bute Street — 26 April 1965

* Closed stations on this line that were in Hertfordshire were Welwyn Garden City (first), Ayot, Wheathampstead and Harpenden East.

Luton Hoo Station, 1 August 1959. This station, known as New Mill End until 1891, especially served Luton Hoo House.

**Luton Hoo Station, looking towards Luton, 5 September 1959.
The goods yard is beyond the level crossing.**

The Great Northern's Dunstable branch, about nine miles of which was in Bedfordshire, originated in the desire of Luton's business elite to connect the town to the railway network. The Luton, Dunstable & Welwyn Junction Railway proposed two routes: one west to the railhead of the London & North Western's Dunstable branch and another south to join the Great Northern near Welwyn. The Dunstable line, although involving considerable construction, went rapidly ahead and opened on 3 May 1858. The more lightly built southern line followed on 1 September 1860. By this time the Luton, Dunstable & Welwyn Junction had merged with the company responsible for building the Great Northern's Hertford branch to form the Hertford, Luton & Dunstable Railway, which was absorbed by the Great Northern in 1861.

The exterior of Luton Hoo Station, 5 September 1959.

The passenger service was varied with branch trains from Hatfield to the London & North Western station at Dunstable, a shuttle service, the 'Skimpot Flyer', between Dunstable and Luton (particularly used by excursionists to the Dunstable Downs), as well as through services to Kings Cross. When the Midland opened its line to London through Luton in 1868, the branch lost its main *raison d'être*. Although the section between Luton and Dunstable remained well used into the 1960s, it was uneconomic due to the short distance involved. The line survived to be converted to diesel haulage, but was closed just a few years later.

Luton Bute Street Station, looking towards Hatfield, 27 March 1954.

Goods traffic was concentrated on the Luton–Dunstable section, Luton Hoo yielding only estate produce, mainly cattle and horses. At Luton the Great Northern had a huge brick warehouse for general goods use, as well as a large coal depot. There were many private sidings including those to a chocolate factory, Laporte's chemical works and Vauxhall Motors' plant. At Dunstable freight came from sidings to a cement works and Waterlows' printing works. In between were further sources of income, which during the First World War included a large munitions plant at Chaul End (for which a short-lived halt was opened). The line south of Luton was closed for goods in 1966, although the Luton–Dunstable section remained to serve an oil depot and cement plant, via a connection laid in with the Midland main line, until 1988.

Luton Bute Street, 7 July 1956. On the left is locomotive No. 69586 with the 8.14 a.m. service to Hatfield, while on the right is No. 44364 with the 7.30 a.m. train from Leighton Buzzard.

The old trackbed from Luton Hoo to Luton is now partly utilised as a country walk. Track on the Luton–Dunstable section remained *in situ* until recently and the stretch has been considered for reopening (Dunstable being the largest town in Britain without a railway station). Although Luton and both Dunstable stations are long demolished, the one at Luton Hoo still stands.

In this picture, taken looking towards Hatfield on 14 April 1962, a railtour of the Stephenson Locomotive Society accounts for the activity at Luton Bute Street. A class J52 0-6-0 No. R47 drew the society special from Hatfield to Luton that day. The huge railway-owned warehouse is on the right.

Dunstable Church Street, *c.*1910. This was renamed Dunstable Town on 1 January 1927.

A view of Dunstable North Station, taken from class 2MT 2-6-2T No. 41222 on 27 March 1954.

Dunstable North, looking towards Hatfield, 24 September 1955. The platform on the right was for terminating trains from Leighton Buzzard.

Locomotive No. 69654, entering Dunstable North with the 5.08 p.m. service from Welwyn Garden City, while a southbound goods train waits for clearance, 24 September 1955.

Dunstable North, looking towards Luton, 14 April 1962. The overgrown platform to the left was probably never used. To the right is the ex-London & North Western goods yard.

Hitchin branch (Bedford to Hitchin)

		Stations closed	Date
Passenger service withdrawn	1 January 1962	Cardington	1 January 1962
Distance	16 miles	Cardington Camp Halt	3 October 1921
Company	Midland	Southill	1 January 1962
		Shefford	1 January 1962
		Henlow Camp	1 January 1962

An ex-Midland Railway 3F 0-6-0 shunting at Henlow sometime in the 1920s. This station was renamed Henlow Camp on 1 March 1933.

For a branch line the Hitchin branch had the least typical origins, for initially it formed part of the Midland's trunk route to London. Prior to the opening of St Pancras in 1868 Midland trains ran by agreement with the Great Northern into Kings Cross via Hitchin. This was a cause of great problems, both operational and financial, to the Midland, and it therefore built its own line into London. The stub portion from Bedford to Hitchin, which along with the route north to Leicester had opened on 8 May 1857, was downgraded to a rural branch line. The branch was never fully up to main line standards, however, for there was a dangerous crossing of the London & North Western's Bedford branch on the level, as well as rather fierce gradients caused by cost cutting. Originally double track throughout, the greater portion was singled in 1911.

Henlow Camp, looking towards Bedford, 18 May 1959.

Branch trains generally operated from the bay platform at Bedford to the up main at Hitchin. The small town of Shefford was the largest on-line community, but Cardington, due to its RAF installations, was probably the most important source of traffic. Indeed, during the First World War traffic was heavy enough to justify the opening of a special halt adjacent to the camp. Officially known as Cardington Workmen's Platform, it was to prove short-lived. Henlow also served an airbase and special leave trains constituted one of the main activities on the line. Southill and Henlow served villages some distance from the stations and therefore cannot have seen much use. Diesel railbus services were introduced on the line in 1958, but were not successful largely due to technical failures and were withdrawn two years later. Light traffic made the line a fairly early victim of closure. The line was well used on the freight side with industrial sidings at Bedford including those to cold storage facilities and grain silos. The area it ran through was mostly devoted to market gardening, especially for the London market. The airbases were also sources of freight traffic. The line was closed to goods in stages from 1963 to 1969. Sections of the old route can still be traced, although the southern half especially has been partially removed. Southill and Cardington stations have been preserved.

Northampton branch (Oakley Junction to Northampton) *

Passenger service withdrawn	5 March 1962	*Station closed*	*Date*
Distance	19.4 miles	Turvey	5 March 1962
Company	Midland		

Turvey Station, 1953.

* The closed station on this line that was in Buckinghamshire was Olney. The closed stations in Northamptonshire were Piddington and Northampton St Johns.

Turvey, looking towards Bedford, 29 March 1954. It was a big station for such a small place!

The Midland's Northampton branch ran from Oakley Junction, about one and a half miles north of Bedford, west to Northampton, and was in many ways a typical rural branch line. Built for a small local company, the Bedford & Northampton Railway, established in the heyday of branch line construction in the mid-1860s, the line opened on 10 June 1872, after some delays presumably caused by the usual shortage of capital. Although it was double track throughout, it did suffer from the severe gradients and curvature illustrative of the low standard of construction of branch lines.

Another view of Turvey from 29 March 1954. Note the London Midland & Scottish 'bulls-eye' signboard and the grounded carriage behind.

After a decade or so the local company was merged into the Midland Railway, which had always worked the line. As was often the case the branch had been enthusiastically constructed in anticipation of extensive traffic that failed to appear, and shared the fate of so many such ventures, becoming a victim of the Beeching era. The greater part of the line was closed for goods not long after passenger closure. The old trackbed has been largely absorbed into the surrounding countryside. About seven miles of the line was in Bedfordshire, the only station on this stretch being Turvey.

Closed stations on lines still open to passengers

Line/service		Stations closed	Date
	Bedford line (Bletchley to Bedford)	Kempston & Elstow Halt	5 May 1941
		Wootton Broadmead Halt	5 May 1941

Wootton Broadmead, looking towards Bedford, 29 September 1967. This opened as a halt on 1 December 1903; the building to the left was the old crossing keeper's house and was typical of others on the line.

The closed Three Counties Station, facing north, 17 September 1974. Originally known as Arlesey Siding until 1 July 1886, this station was then renamed Three Counties and closed in 1959. It was reopened as Arlesey Station on 3 October 1988.

The closed Arlesey Station, 17 September 1974.

ARLESEY

Stations closed	*Date*
Chiltern Green	7 April 1952
Bedford Midland Road	30 September 1978

Stations closed	*Date*
Ampthill	4 May 1959
Oakley	15 September 1959
Sharnbrook	2 May 1960

Jubilee class locomotive No. 5644 with a down perishables service at Chiltern Green Station, 13 July 1939.

Chiltern Green, looking towards London, 27 August 1955.
This station opened on 13 July 1868.

Class 2MT 2-6-2 No. 41270 taking on water at Bedford Midland Road Station, 25 September 1955. This was resited and replaced by the current Bedford Station on 30 September 1978.

Ampthill Station, looking towards Bedford, 13 April 1959. The canopies on the right were a typical feature of Midland stations.

Ampthill Station, 13 April 1959.

Oakley Station, looking south. Originally the first station north of Bedford, this opened on 8 May 1857.

Oakley Station. A row of coal offices lies beyond the neat station gardens.

Oakley Station, 13 April 1954. Note the architectural similarity with Henlow Station (p. 26).

The signal box at Oakley, looking towards Kettering, 13 April 1959.

Sharnbrook Station, *c.*1905.

Sharnbrook, 13 April 1959.